MYCOCOSMIC

Poems

Mycocosmic

POEMS

Lesley Wheeler

TUPELO PRESS

North Adams, Massachusetts

ISBN: 978-1-961209-16-9 (PAPER)
LCCN 2024945279

Tupelo Press
P.O. Box 1767, North Adams,
Massachusetts 01247
(413) 664–9611 / editor@tupelopress.org
www.tupelopress.org

Tupelo Press is an award-winning independent
literary press that publishes fine fiction, nonfiction,
and poetry in books that are a joy to hold as well as
read. Tupelo Press is a registered 501(c)(3) nonprofit
organization, and we rely on public support to carry
out our mission of publishing extraordinary work
that may be outside the realm of the large commercial
publishers. Financial donations are welcome and are
tax deductible.

COVER ART:
Pearl Cowan, "Radiant Void," 2023. Watercolor gouache and ink on
paper, 10"x 8". Used by permission of the artist.

Cover and text design by Dede Cummings

Contents

for Claire

. . . the uncontrolled lives of mushrooms are a gift—and a guide—when the controlled world we thought we had fails.

—Anna Lowenhaupt Tsing

Had nature an Apostate— / That Mushroom—it is Him!

—Emily Dickinson

What permits us to love one another and the earth we inhabit is that we and it are impermanent. We obsolesce. Life's everlasting. Individuals aren't.

—John Cage

So many of us!/ So many of us!

—Sylvia Plath

MYCOCOSMIC

Poems

We Could Be

mycelial, eating toxins together,
decomposing what's still indigestible
about this place. The singed taste.
Could spread our soiled hands wide,
vegetate, infiltrate, collaborate.
Below ground, we could grow
fat on loss, bust out in the wildest
shapes. Puffball. Flagellate.
Our mistakes gorgeous in dispersal
across polluted skies. Help me try.

After a fire, fungi emerge, pyrophiles who may lurk in mosses & lichens

Extended Release

The oxy hardly works at all. The refrigerator
rings like a telephone. I hold her hand as another
nonhealer unwraps and anoints her flaming sores.
Sores isn't right. They're craters or portals
she keeps slipping through: hospital, rehab,
hospital, home. The visiting nurse, with whom
I've fallen in love, whispers to my mother,
You're so strong—she's too tired to laugh—
and to me, *You're doing a good job.* I could weep
but I don't. My mother keeps yelling into the landline,
Somebody's at the door! I trash sour milk
and a rotting pepper from the bottom drawer.
She points at the ceiling whirlpools and asks,
What do you think I'll wear up there? I dress
her in a clean fleece nightgown. She feels so cold.
Soon she can't lift her bruised hands. I call 911.
When she opens her eyes to the EMT she cries,
Oh, Les, what have you done. Each new doctor halts
the prayer of oxycodone. I should have brought pills,
but I won't know how to daughter till I'm done.
I swear that refrigerator's haunted. I'm writing this
poem I'll never be able to read aloud after another
transfer. *Can I have a bed,* she says, while lying in one.
She's in quarantine but I hear she's refusing Ensure
and those tiny cubed peaches, tender as blisters.
She always thought people had a right to end
their suffering. She never believed in heaven.

---

for years—spore get *stimulated* *by these disturbances,*

But I'm not going to that other, she tells me,
raising the skin where her eyebrows would have been.
What's your favorite place? she asks. I smell
the ringing edge of the ocean. Hers is a garden.
But there can be a garden near a beach, I say,
full of tropical flowers, we can be neighbors.
She might smile under palm fronds there, lit
by hibiscus, full-bellied and finally warm.

---

fruiting to bring the forest back.[1]

[ruin eaters]

Sex Talk

After a fight, men want to have sex, but I don't, my mother said.
She glanced at undergraduate me from the driver's seat as if a
    membrane

had been breached and asked, *Do you?*

                                    I wanted to change the subject.
We were returning from the mall through the stony suburb

where the model lived, the one who said, *Nothing comes between me
and my Calvins*, where the fire department floods the common

every winter for skating, creating warty ice ungroomed by
    Zambonis,
grass snagged in its skin like ingrown hairs. My mother kept
    looking

at me, her eye a sideways question mark, tricky liquid liner painted
along the lid, pupil unrelenting.

                            Everyone in the family except

my mother owned their own lockable room. She had to read her
    Harlequins
out in the open like a gazelle. We stalked through, asking and
    asking:

Doesn't everyone hope
            believe some secret power
                        gallant angel will resurrect them

where is the, why can't I, help me. Nightly her shirtless husband
arrived with a pump-jar of Jergens demanding she moisturize his
    back,

scaly from chlorine, but I knew—spy crouching on the stairs,
fingertips brushing wallpaper embossed with creamy trees,

its surface all bubbles and seams—what he was after.

Once at a Modernism conference a guy chased me around the
    canapes

while lecturing me on Marianne Moore's asexuality.
I knew my mother didn't like sex, but I never asked

was it generally or just sex with my father. Nothing
gets between me and my shame.

I don't know what Moore wanted,
just that she wrote cryptic poems under her mother's surveillance.

Heterosexual marriage: she, too, disliked it. She was nearly sixty
when her mother died.

                    Now I know death's intimacy.

How honesty frightens me. My mother is everywhere:
cells lodged in my body, invisible flakes of skin on sweaters,

a baggie of ashes on the bookshelf.

---

after the conflagration? As if saving's shadow work is beyond

                              Not after a fight.
Until adrenaline burns off, I'm hot the wrong way. Clenched.

I hope she knew what an orgasm feels like. (During my first,
a rainbow tree grew between me and my eyelids, privately.)

She said to us, over her book, *No, I don't want
to hug you goodnight.*

---

human strength & wit.
                    Call the fungi in. But there is no *beyond*—

Gran Torino Gigan

Like crawling into a forest at night, that station-
wagon, as piney, as vast. Branches shushing.

You could spend your entire childhood
in the way-back. Buzzes fade up front,
where beltless adults murmur and smoke

after unfurling musty sleeping bags
in the trunk, mine printed red, white, and blue

in rhizomatic zigzags, with a sharp zipper.
Numberless cousins nested there, lulled

to sleep as soon as the big car creaked
onto the parkway, green like a pine forest

of the mind. Unfurled on a musty sleeping bag,
I wouldn't sleep for years. The stars
are such old ideas, suggesting patterns but

refusing to connect the dots. Tomorrow rumbles
beneath us all. I can hear it when no one talks.

---

no waste—everything is here and edible. [being & burning & aftermath]
Mycelium describes the most common of fungal habits, better thought of not

Garden State

A man in a suit approached and touched my arm.
Would I pose in front of the merry-go-round?
I was thirteen, free for an hour in the middle
of Paramus Park Mall, in America. I was America.
The man was leading a tour; the tourists spoke
no English. My English mother said, *Your sister
is beautiful, but you are reasonably attractive.*
She chose my clothes, that day a blouse abuzz
with flowers, a pink pleated skirt. Yes, I said,
and sat on the bench. Everybody smiled. My hair
curled like orchid petals. A carousel horse whispered,
Why would they point their cameras at you?
As if you were pretty. This will be a story, I replied.
Of cold glass eyes that saw the bloom in me.

---

as a thing but as a process: an exploratory,
              irregular tendency,

Dark Energy

Root-brain speculates into
soil, hyphae nosing toward
rot, digesting that we are many—
stranded & one-bodied,
the ten thousand sexes of our
fungal computer penetrating
rock & plant & cloud & animal or
becoming indistinguishable from
what was called individual,
fed ideas & feeding them back,
symbiotic now whether or not
we notice kindness fruiting
each rainy morning, red caps
beside steep branching trails
sheeted into streams as the mountain
drains, it is so full of feeling—
you have to wonder what futures
each mushroom lifts into being,
tender manifestoes inscribed in gills,
& how they will disperse—but
they are dispersing, believe it—
long live the revolution of spore!—
the drive to choose with intelligence
how to wind around obstacles
and survive together, mycelial
filigree exerting the pressure
of fifty atmospheres, not monument-
building but persistent, mysterious,
the hungry electrical process of love!

---

writes Merlin Sheldrake. [2]
          A maybe ^{or} a knotty curiosity—

Peri-Aubade

You sweat yourself awake after sexy
dreams about verb contractions,
flap the comforter while on the skin side
of flame-painted plaster a real
wind rises, thumbing
the tin roof like a smoker who
cannot get the house to stay alight.

Out there, rain-fed fungus bursts
through the universal veil.
Who knew that each hot flash
would arrive with a whistle of doom
so keen it would jerk you out of sleep?
Not you. Not the swollen dawn.
Maybe ghostpipes did, noun

become verb as they mushroom
every muggy morning, flinging off kin.
Maybe the wind knows, with its freight—
train ardor and friction, blowing
bulletins about the mystery you are—
you are and you will be—you hotly
were and hotly now you are

The living seam by which much of the world is stitched into relation...[3]

Oxidation Story

The body bled for seven weeks before
succumbing to the surgeon, who torched
the nursery like a mob of angry villagers.
You bet they're angry. Everybody's angry.
Physiological indices of anger include
rose-tinted vision, muffled hearing, rapid
heartrate, and perceived distension of time.
Some epinephrine sharpens recall; too much
impairs it. Does a doctor like to burn patients?
The body can't remember. The body likes anger,
the livid exhilaration, not so much
the landscape after. Once the body, aching,
made an appointment with a psychic.
He wore a shirt imprinted with a wolf.
When he lay down the cards, he said,
Good things come to you through fire.
The body hot-flashes, remembering months
it bled and weakened. How it stank of smoke.
Now the body is a ruin haunted by a girl
of twelve. Over and over she finds the first
red smear and phones her mother, who cries,
I'm sorry. The villagers never say *I'm sorry.*
The body searches through embers for something
good. It feels sorry for the girl, with so
much to dread until chemistry releases her.

Less a flame

More a swarm than a single bee.

Less a poem

An Underworld

I stopped my breath for as long as I could
in the grit beneath my little brother's bed,
afraid of my father. Even the dust would
betray me if it dared, and what then?
Pupils so flared a kid could hide in there.
My mother loved but wouldn't save us
or didn't believe there was a passage out.
My father's laughter scattered hail.
His step cracked rifts in the ground.
So, shadow, what should I have done?
Words make no shelter, lone or shared.
Left him, left them, the darkness says.

than an underground library lending out speculating hyphae

Map Projections

When my father died,
I said to my sister,
I'm sorry I let
him do that to you.

My sister said, *No.*
I wasn't even on his radar.
He didn't think I
was worth it.
He aimed for you.

· · ·

nutrients
that translate messages via electrochemical pulses & learn

A peninsula of cabinets
divided kitchen from dining room.
My father sat at one end of the table.
In my memory's seating plan,
I claimed the furthest
chair, stranding my sister
in range of his hands.

      I don't know why we called
      the kitchen peninsula an island.
      My mother blockaded herself behind
      it with my brother's highchair,
      as if she could save only one.

• • •

                           around obstacles.
[they absolutely learn] by nosing

Meanwhile my sister, marooned.

It's as vivid to me as a history book.

My father slapped her head
during the hostage crisis,
after his double martini, and
under Reagan, dry-drunk
on the Atkins plan,
greasy from chewing five
naked unsalted burgers
fuming on the plate.

           I can travel back
           through corridors of shag
           and chart it all: the mock-
           Tudor Styrofoam beams wishing
           they could support the ceiling,
           the stink of fried meat,
           the sting of how he flicked
           her skull, middle finger snapping
           past a thumb that pretended
           to want to restrain it.
           It hurt more than you'd think.

• • •

Fungi pair with other creatures cell to cell
                   to tendril—

Wait, whose skull? Disorienting.
The truth is a shoreline. It moves.
I wonder which of us he loved enough
to give latitude to or fix in sight.

• • •

bartering & bantering [*we have no idea what a species is*[4]]—if

I always wanted to live
on an archipelago.

. * *

they're symbionts. The rest—decomposers—stop death

My pulse still bangs at the dinner hour.
The word island makes me think of my mother,
a compass rose who wheeled off the edge of the map.

---

from overwhelming the living. [undone so many]

The Underside of Everything You've Loved

The woman I wanted sat in front of me in class.
I used to speak French. We were reading *Madame Bovary*.

She'd torn her tee down the back. My pupils shrank
against the glow of her skin. I gave up the language.

Once I kissed a different girl—we were girls then—calling it
practice. When later we passed on the street, her face sang

and I pretended not to know the verses.
I had two loves separate, expatriate H.D. told Freud

and me in a book I read extracurricularly because a man
suggested it, the man I'd marry, who committed to lifelong study

of the radiant words trapped in my mouth. Meanwhile
I wrote a senior thesis on Adrienne Rich's metaphors

for intimacy: vomiting together, in "Twenty-One Love
Poems"; pregnancy; volcanoes choking on lava.

One of the loves I denied was named for a tree. Another, a bird.
People say I'm reserved, but poems can't keep secrets.

They double everything. Luckily no one can translate them.
I'm a lucky person. Books and the man who loved me saved me

Some commensal decomposers are infamous for other

when I wanted to die, which doesn't erase the dimples beside her spine.
Now I research fungi, who sometimes reproduce sexually

and sometimes otherwise. People die for love. I
didn't fear losing as much as owning my desires.

Maybe I would have walked across a forested border,
if I'd never met him, into another country.

Maybe it doesn't matter. Maybe I am only matter.
My cells have changed, since then, almost entirely. What I regret

is turning my back on the torch song in the laurel
in panic so earsplitting it exiled me.

kinds of magic
      spirit-work: soothing wrath & grief in humans, disintegrating toxic feelings.

Smart

At twenty-five, adrift in the mirror,
I cried, *It will never get better than this!*
Shocked, then laughing, as if a time-lapse film
unblossomed in the rented sheen
of the medicine cabinet. The girlishness
I was told to tend ready to crisp and drop.
That's what pretty does. It dies.
So I shrugged off pretty, despite
my mother's warnings, and chose
a cheap wedding dress that quit
at the knee and loosely shrouded
the most suitable I'd ever be. Refused
to process in regalia for my PhD.
Smart shatters the vase.
Smart skips the strappy heels.
Smart enough to learn I would never
matter to my father except
as I reflected him, I gathered
bouquets of promotions and pages,
each stained by pistils under pressure
for years. Now I'm a litter of leaves
molding in a specimen jar.
Through the bottle protecting me,
I see how often it's the pretty one
gilded by honors. The irony.
It's not that I picked the wrong
way to please. My eyes just smart.
It's the cell walls breaking down.

Researchers describe *movement of feelings from separateness to
interconnectedness…
catharsis…forgiveness.* [5]

Venus / Dodo

In the galleries of glassy-eyed extinct birds,
plumage wilts and talons grip dead limbs.
Nothing to sing about. So why is my skin
humming? A floor below the dodo, revelation:
small as a woman's palm, the misnamed Venus
of Willendorf, ocher-tinted limestone
heartthrob. My fists tighten. Can't look away,
although a paparazzo is annoyed
I'm lingering in his frame, shamelessly.

She's magnetic. Focal / marginal. Defunct /
droning on. Venus, I hear you're woman-made,
faceless, proportioned like someone gazing down
at breasts and belly. It's lovely how matter claims room.
Excavating space before melting into the slash.
Anonymous / enormous. I am. I am.

—the savior thing. Hope can be suspect, sustaining, ruinous, & right.

[shapeshifter]

Self-Portrait / Golden Shovel

Climbing out of decomposition, I
realized I was viscous. None could hold
me unless her hands were glass. My
cradle was a wheelbarrow. Honey
envied how I would not crystallize. And
I continue to flow although as yet I
resist dissolution; my molecules store
what the bees once said; on the trowel, my
rain's in beads; my dough will not be bread.
Is this a woman thing? A kitchen's in
my mind, some butternut puree, a little
plot of dirt, six by six by two. Sorry if that jars
you. I'll always say sorry, sorry and
spoil the ceiling anyway, leak down cabinets
because I burst the pipe with the pressure of
let's call it feeling or maybe shiftiness, my
reluctance to insist, although I will.

Fungi are famous for changing shape in relation to their encounters and environment[6]

Harrowing

When I tender cash for shiny baby turnips,
the farmer steps back, afraid. The sky looks
plush, but softness is non-essential.
The foodbank begs for volunteers. I take a shift,
strain my back, retreat to stare at a calendar
washed white as a vegetable the root of whose name
is revolution. The owners of closed stores deadhead
pansies to prettify unpeopled streets
as people sicken, refusing to save or be saved.
These days are like, what even are they like?
Ruptured soil. Ruin. Meanwhile, bulbs mull
their underground life, how it sharpens them.

—self is relation. My daughter says, *You're not ready for magic mushrooms*
even as literary auto-experiment. Her alarm convinces me—for now—

Deferred

Look at the mountain, find my boots, abandon
      walls, look at the mountain. It's all I do.
The president tweets *DACA is dead* while
      the magnolia publishes other news: the future
will be pink. Whom should I listen to?
      Beets for lunch. Do not think of my father,
who loved them, as juice bleeds over the salad. Do not
      remember my mother-in-law, whose jewelry
I wear, teardrops strung along a chain.
      She died far away, last verses unheard.
It's a hard, it's a hard, it's a hard rain's a-gonna fall,
      he plays, the curator of beatness who
visits class with Dylan on cue. Scratches
      under scratches. No one's allowed to dream
anymore. A student comes by with poems and fear
      of deportation. So many words; so few.
Evening, home, where once I found on the lawn
      a note from neo-nazis. Look at the mountain,
crowned in rose. *Where black is the color and none*
      is the number, the singer foretold. Still I talk,
fail to talk, and grant some songs their visas.
      And look at the mountain, its gloomy hunch, its glow.

---

not to disturb a trembling lightless substrate. Don't know what figments
                                        filaments

In Weird Waters Now

Noun: destiny; power. *Weird swept*
them away (Morris and Wyatt, 1895
translation of *Beowulf*). The past

is a noisy cataract. Don't even try
to resist it. Second definition, adjective:
Shakespeare didn't mint the Weird Sisters

rhyming over a cauldron but he did
bestir them, spinning a wayward descriptive
on the current his tongue paddled.

Having or claiming power. That
tastes good. Yet the rocks over which
my country rages are more like

unfathomably sinister. I always
get stranded here, in a rhizome of horror
that can't bear weight, turning bitter words

over in my mouth. *The person*
of the house gave a weird little laugh
(Dickens, 1865). You must, unless you plan

---

of tiny intention prowl around in there. Meanwhile, mycophilic types declare,

to people the weird places of the earth
with weird beings (Kingsley, 1866),
emigrating to Canada. Third arrives

the verb: to preordain; to warn of fate.
I wierd ye, gangna there! (Jamieson,
1806). I'm going scared. I'm afeared,

beyond weirded out. I'm choking
on the *weirding peas* used in divination.
My mother warned me bad things

come in threes so watch your feet—
don't cross on the stairs, don't talk
to strange men, never spill salt unless

you want to weep. Uncanny laughter
bubbles disturbingly. I need your weird,
sisters, because these are troubled seas.

[W]e must use these organisms to steer, repair and rebuild our stressed

You Know Where the Smithy Stood by the Clinkers

No plaque remembers William,
son of John Anderson, although
together they forged nails, spikes,
& crossties to brace an antebellum
Classical Revival porticoed building
whose cupola uplifts a white statue,
whose belly is lined by museum cases
& donor names engraved in marble.

None of their ironwork is visible but
bootscrapes: four handmade bars
bracketed by looping upstrokes,
fern-curled flourishes on signatures
few trouble to read. I study them,
which does not scrape me clean.

---

yet *faithful celestial transport*[7] [Earth I guess] —fungal factories for food,

Submicroscopic

A virus wants to replicate. It hates
to be lonesome. A virus wants to replicate
its genome, refold, virally reiterate
all a virus knows in its folds, helical, prolate—
in all the viral morphologies. Not great
for a nonviral body, these revelries, late-
night recombinations gathering mutations
while tonight's desperate combo plays, but

hear it viral style. Genes will duplicate.
A pathogen's life, if a gene relocation
machine really lives, is brief. It can't wait
or fabricate more than a minor song. One pleated
sonnet; no crown. If there's love, you can't watch
it spike. Yet it wants. In its whisper, a catch.

biofoam, anti-inflammatories, purification & the fixation of carbon

Forecasts Can Be Invocations

Snow, vote down that grass.
Snow, hush the root-shifted
vehemence of sidewalk slabs.

Please bring your storm watch.
Your vortex. Your crystal.
Your level. Your holy knack

for flake and stick and blanket.
Pile and pile on transmission lines.
Snow, fall among us and

in my bothered mind. I'm calling
you, snow, and beginning to wonder
if supercool silence is your reply.

---

or lead contamination! [make & unmake me] [heal & blister]

Flammable Almanac

I pick up the cards as a kind of game
because the pages of my calendar are salt.
A char-cloaked man who spilled
three cups hunkers in me, unable
to budge. The air smells like smoke.

Put your toes in the water, Temperance
says. I know you're discouraged but
the only way you will ever arrive
is to get your feet wet. Bury bulbs;
one day they will be lilies in your pocket.

So I armor up and ride across a desert
upside down, wand erect,
so enflamed my horse is blushing.
There may be nowhere to go
but I move fast through and past

summer, my hands learning the meanings
as the meanings learn me. An ashy history
flows into an egg-yolk tomorrow.
Autumn I become the King of Pentacles.
Ivy climbs the ground, the chair, and fruits

all over my clothes. When the psychic said,
Good things come to you through fire,
I thought he meant my whole world had to burn.
Now I know the fire reddens inside me.
Every paper window incandescent.

Hippocrates recommended the amadou mushroom for cauterization

For Metamorphosis, with Bibliomancy

Nightingale, Paisley Rekdal

This is the season for transmutation. Change
began some time ago: electrical storms,
dreams grinding slow like brass gears. An icebox
sighs; you're grateful. Around each bruise, each sign
inscribed in purple and teal, a halo forms.
You rattle dice and roll seventeen. What
could that mean—almost woman and certainly
prey? Rattle the news but your horoscope is blank.
Rattle a page and a person falls out, a fleshy
hag in linen pants, near enough you catch
the ozone scent. *The woman stands, straightens,*
and you see her mouth thin to a not unpleasant line...
Well, you wanted monstrousness. Leathery
rind unwinding. This is the season for transmutation.

& Ötzi the Ice Man carried it. Trip on it, worship it, marry it.
Store your bitcoin in Mycelium™.

Rhapsodomancy
Major Arcana

0. Every time you speak, you're dancing at the edge of a cliff.

I. Just seize the mic, ignoring the pong of scorched plastic. You will burn your candle at both ends and never die.

II. Be pomegranate. Come on, try.

III. Mantra: you are not everyone's mother. This is an epoch of abundance. Scarf it down.

IV. There's a dick in your life. Could it be an inner dick? If you live by the clock, break it.

V. So many futures to reveal, so many truths to tell yourself. In the meantime, whatever your temple, bring it flowers. You crave the groove of holy music.

VI. Volcanoes are fertile and aflame. Choose what you love—or love not to choose.

VII. The stars may bloom in daylight and sphinxes adore you, but you'd better keep your hieroglyphic armor on.

VIII. Maintain a firm grip on that red snout. Some fail to observe your magnetism, given the headrush of roses.

Amadou is also tinder, the spongy swirly striped horse hoof fungus that grows on birches & conifers.

IX. Dusk is swooning. Today will be resinous: rosemary, lavender.

X. See what happens when you ask a poem for advice? Every word is a chimera. All you can do is ride it.

XI. Expect an acid verdict from a sharp-tongued woman. Swallowing it may sting your throat.

XII. Upside, flipside: what crucifies you is also alive.

XIII. Don't freak out. Desire always dies.

XIV. Pour yourself a glass of something expensive. Now share it.

XV. You didn't need wine in the first place, you thirsty thing.

XVI. It seems like lightning forks down from the sky, but it leaps from the ground to knock you out. Life will zap your hat off with a thrumming sound.

XVII. There's always a risk, yet if you pour out your nakedness, you just might shine.

XVIII. Appreciate that you are pulled into tides by a satellite.

XIX. Backed against a wall, you thrive.

Fungi eat charcoal although they prefer
　　　　　the tasty insects

XX. Roll your liquid eyes at prophecies, but the angel still arrives.

XXI. Float up and enjoy some perspective. You know how fireflies alight as they rise? That's beautiful you, luminescing.

---

that wildfire explodes—mycelium is ravenous. Mycelium goes mad

Counterphobic

Pondering *defixiones*—curse tablets and binding spells
inscribed on thin lead sheets—during the weak-tea days
of late November, whiskered familiar pretending to sleep,
balding plastic raven grouching on the bookshelf, a person
might feel a chthonic force stir to whisper that *words
are amulets, busyness a counterspell*, all of it hopeless to ward off
the blurred lumbering works of a brain calculating risk
like a stream that eats at the foundations of what's perched above,
fragile but trying to act normal. A person might wonder
why scratched phylacteries rarely surprise. They say, *Please
spare me or make X suffer the pain he dealt, but threefold.
I bind X chiasmatically!* Hair, nails, and effigies
optional. Every book a cemetery. Every prayer a well.
Letters rolled, folded, sealed with the address of supernatural power
or the restless dead. It might seem futile to keep at it.
Sometimes I think so, too. The ritual is desperate but maybe also
blessed—to name the hurts engraved in me then chuck them
away.

---

like other buried geniuses. It promotes cryptic lifestyles. Neither spells

For Evaporation of Hope, with Bibliomancy
Japanese Tales, Royall Tyler

Best to admit they never loved you, these strangers
among whom you lived and worked, these dear
damaged machines, creaking with the labor
of dragging their shadows around. They were built
of bewitched manuscripts and cold tea bags.
They were not humans at all but frightful demons!
They were too sad even to notice your hurt.
Rainbows straggle across muddy puddles: olive,
ocher, teal, marooned. Some call it perspective,
what happens when the demons wheel toward
a congealed horizon, but they are actually shrinking,
become dolls in the game you never weary
of playing. Set them down gently and strip off
that reenactor's costume. Sun-scent stings like a
marigold's. Aridity clacks against morning clouds.
Best to admit they never loved you, these strangers.

---

nor spore can fix every err

or. When Paul Stamets says in a documentary[8]

Early Cretaceous Swims Up to the Bar

For weeks a part of me stayed
at current's edge, peering down,
dark to dark, pondering
the phosphorescent gar haunting
the Hillsborough River, although

sources said there was no such thing.
The memory stayed on like ink
or hankering. Enigma snouted
and stalked inside me, nocturnal,
torpedo-shaped dun submerged

relic, ganoid scales impenetrable,
its fossil of a nose aglow.
A smallish alligator gar, surely,
exciting tiny bioluminescent
creatures by its skulking,

ignoring the greenish flash
as, always hungry, it strives
to plug that spiral valve intestine
with gizzard shad, unsuspecting
waterfowl, stray engine parts.

Its emptiness fills me. Frank
appetite with a double row
of obscure teeth, magnificent,
indifferent to light. If only I
could wear a skin of fire.

---

of mycelium,
that we are descendants
it is the mother of us all, that shrooms are not

Memorandum of Understanding

I believe in utility poles, transformers,
lightning arrestors. Subtransmission lines
and static lines. The dead southern yellow pine

on the corner and its arcane spiral symbols.
I've woken to a stranger murmuring my name.
Once, in a rented house, a ghost girl saying *help me*.

I wear earring chandeliers of scavenged fox bones.
I've never seen white hands in the dark, except mine.
I once caught the signal of a running man,

a dimness near the moving boxes in my antebellum
office building. There's blood in the walls.
I don't know about spirits. I believe in trying

to talk but mostly in listening. Power cables
are insulated by the air itself. Overhead
it mumbles and sometimes shrieks.
I can feel its tendrils reaching for me.

---

party drugs but medicines & sacraments, I think about having & being

It Is Advantageous to Place on the Table
a [Hollow Figurine] of Apollo, with Bibliomancy
Greek Magical Papyri in Translation Including
the Demotic Spells, *by Hans Dieter Betz*

The angry woman, thrice passed over,
should first procure a table of olive wood
and carve upon it in a circle a secret word,
abjuring for three days any uncleanness
and eating no lichen, to please the gods. Next
she must ink the sacred Project Description
onto a seven-leaved sprig of laurel and summon
three referees, anointing them with honey.
When all is ready, *recite this formula toward the sunrise,*
offering dark wine: I am brilliant and deserving.
Give unto me the fellowship. If she burns
the inscribed branch and stuffs its ashes into
the drive of a blue computer, disregarding
its sighs, acceptance will come in spring, when
she may pass this charm to another angry woman.

---

protective
a mother not always bioluminescent
kind. Plus animals are *multispecies composites*[9]

Particle-Wave

People radiate light they cannot see.
The subatomic universe blazes with chances.
Wants momentum. Defies divisibility.
There is no safe road through misery's ocean,
so light elects another trajectory. Sunshine rages
on the rocks, which may or may not feel
the beat. That's fine. Observer, step in.
The breakers will rise and release anyway,
particles of grit finding their shine.
You could be part of their experiment
knocking at the edge of certainty.

---

hard to assemble in linear order. My branching I are of my mother,

Eighteen

My baby is hunting for evil Sierpinsky numbers.

My baby unwraps his number theory sock and
turns it into a hungry puppet, cocked like an ostrich.

My baby explains modular arithmetic to the math club

while they perspire in their billboard tees. My baby
wears billboard tees in the fight against innumeracy.

My baby will convert you to binary as soon as look

at your analogue face. How many ohs lurk inside you,
how many lonely ones? My baby knows the answer

and is sorry but won't say it, not today, not out loud,

digits too sharp inside his ticker, an adult's heart,
a gift bag, an ungraphable solution to the countdown

years whose number he owns.

---

her cells survive in me although, like ghosts, they're too small to see.

Rusty

Industrious bird, erect on the fence:
all evening our phones have chirred.
Words without words. My son
could not solve it. At the crux
of a rug's complex design, he stood
around, mute, alive. Asleep I opened
the cellar door and out streamed
a clutch of baby turtles, green
as April, dream-shells still tender.
I had to defend them from cats,
keep safe a path for everyone,
and, robin, I'm not sure I can.
This morning the clouds are low
and the wind is damp. You hunt
with a practical eye, minding a catbird's
nagging, a dove's endless fluting
why. My son sleeps, in theory.
Tonight, prom, when he'll shrug
his father's old tuxedo on and
huddle for numberless photographs.
I suppose you, red as a brick,
will settle into a nest of mud,
wishing hope would never fail,
although, sometimes, it does.

When Robert Macfarlane writes that *[d]eep time awareness might*

Unsonnet

When color comes back to the world,
leaving gets near. By the roadside, auburn
and cream cows chew spangled green.
Creeks steam. A lone bull's horns gore
my heart. Judas trees in flower blur.
Scintillant mist unveils an omen
of mountains. Rows of trees divide
each pasture, branches spread wide,
because they never needed to compete
for light. Please, fog, roll back over
my life. Shrink, leaves, to your old
sites inside secret wood. May days be short
and expeditions brief. No spring. No grief.

---

help us see ourselves as part of a web of gift
inheritance
and legacy[10]

Doubled, Briefly

Finally, I consider whether
I have been a terrible mother.
A squirrel limps by, too wilted
for chatter. I might just be.

I would wake early, Saturdays,
worried for one or the other—
decibel of fever-cry, a swell
of friendless misery—

because I'd been too tired
all week to register trouble
or fix what was mendable.
Crow-feather; slant pine tree.

Mirror of lapses; hot spell simmers.
This love is hardly bearable.

---

mycelium thinks, sure. But unlike plants, fungi have no wish to catch a human eye—

Half-Life

It's the eve of New Year's Eve. The doctor won't
    phone back. No one would who hasn't lived

inside the lightning—cascades of jaw-rattling power—
    minor local seizures each time I turn my head.

One capsule left. Would swallowing it help?
    It sparks in my palm. The answering service,

built to disperse a patient's transmissions, won't forward
    my calls until a signal delay multiplies my cackle

psychiatrically. The expert in discontinuation syndrome
    prescribes an electrical switch, a fuel break

between antidepressants while the wildfires fizzle.
    Problem is, self are the insulation and the voltage.

The burn and the landscape it remakes. As the new
    drug rewires self, self wonders if brain zaps

are angers ganging up on synapses, hurdling what?
    Firelines, firewalls, some rocky thing. Now

the shocks are metaphors, a healthy omen, if mixed.
    Time to pick up what's wrecked. Arrange rubble

in a circuit or a ring. Self is both the blaze and its wary tender,
    so scorched and tender, a dizzy split and splitting thing.

---

as Michael Pollan says, *Mushrooms don't give a shit.*[11] [even when
                                        they sprout from it]

Sore Tongue Song

Among the features of normal people that I am lacking are
four adult molars. Absence runs in my family. For two decades,
four baby teeth resisted until their roots began to dissolve.
One shattered during a birthday dinner to warn me. I schooled
the others to show more grit. With every X-ray, the survivors
dwindled, ever more shadowy, deformed. Finally, near my fiftieth
Christmas, a second baby molar shivered into chunks. Collapse
runs in my family. Cadaver-bone was sutured into my jaw, a post
drilled, molds taken, substitute glued into yellowing ranks. The
surgeon sang "Uptown Girl." Optimism does not run in my family.
The replacement is too large and juts into the cave where my
tongue wants to sleep. Every morning, a pink muscle protests. We
don't want to inhabit me. I am sorry, I tell my tongue. Abyss is our
inheritance. And persistence.

Not showy. Not ambitious.

[not furious not grieving] —Hungry. Fungi devour people

Giant Tube Worm

Dear rift-dweller thriving
without light by hydrothermal vents
in hostile ocean abyssal zones

amid smoking chimneys spewing
danger that would wither anybody else:
cheers for living a thousand years

secreting chitin, you single and
plural aggregation of winners
tangling roots promiscuously

with other invertebrates, never mind
the lack of mouth, gut, or anus
since you lean on symbionts

who help you chemosynthesize
while your scarlet flag,
sole exposed tongue of flesh,

licks up like a sexy nub of lipstick.
Way to handle pressure.
Yet your rotten-egg stench—

emitted not by waste that, given
your anuslessness, has a way
of piling up, but by sulfides

---

tugging their molecules apart
        & returning them to the *detrital food chain.*[12]

in your blood—has reached me,
poison-lover excreting toxins!
I refuse to become you.

I know you feed on sunlessness.
My grandfather's shunning
of my mother, before cancer

invaded the shade of his cranium.
My mother's years sleepwalking
through rainbow grocery stores,

driving home without the baby,
an accident squalling in the cart.
Your endurance is an art, but watch

how I cut myself loose, raising a red
branchial plume to say goodbye,
chemoautotrophic deep. Suffering

is not my due.

Tricky mimics, they kill as well as cure. Meet each carefully & ask: do you wish

Family Tree

The third wife served my father divorce papers
on his deathbed, desperate and on the scent
of rolls of carrion fifties she hadn't trusted to the bank.
He'd buried them to feed the stinking sumac.

The third wife's sister and my sister got pissed
at his funeral. I thought it might come to fists
so I murmured gentle things—I'm quiet, in person—

but my sharp-shinned hawk of a sister was right
to scream from the branches. Years later, we should
have smelled something when our brother,
sole executor of our mother's will, stalled.

We spent, god, almost two years in calls. Tree
of heaven. He couldn't stop squeezing small change.

Now I keep pleading with my mother's ash:
you lived with them, fed them, laundered their clothes.
How could you not know? Two men wasting

so much love. But my father's suckering ailanthus
cloned itself in my brother, and I'm my mother,
shopping for potions to clean the fury up.

---

to nourish me?
    blow my delusions of individuality?
    end my life? Fungi, plants, & animals compete & collaborate. Again

Convertible Moon
  for Judy

Locked to sleep alone in a lidded crib, she
shook and screamed in the key of starlight, desperate
to slip the gear into drive: one, two, three, a
billion and breakout.

Decades flew and she forgot how to count. Why.
Revving, launching, slamming the wall, but mystified.
Come her last trapped new year, the moon so fine, so
near, she begged a ride.

No one heard her open the door and vault into
shine. She rode that wolf moon away. I hope
she knew. I hope she lit up the highway. Every
molecule set loose.

[have I lost the thread] it comes back to relation: whisper a syllable &

Double the Ingredients

Inside motherhood, fearfulness replicates
incurably. She made me of pain, with pain.

Chemo cured her when pain unmade her
but now she risks infection for groceries.

Risks the virus reaching for frozen peas
with crooked hands. She dreads everything but death

and its crooked grin. Dread bends me too. Not
of my death—my will to keep going wobbles

like a shaky wheel on a shopping cart—but hers.
Theirs. I unravel like her. I nearly break.

Since those knotless days my babies broke free
of the love I hoarded, love I hid sometimes

like canned goods in my cupboard heart, dread
propagates. Inside these days, I'm mothering fear.

------

it may not change a god's mycelial mind but must alter the whisperer

Mail-Order LaCharta

Buy her tarts and a lavender
teacake with lemon. Order
a Christmas pudding to set on fire,
some forties swing, shrink-wrapped carols
      from the Three Tenors. Then ship her
      honeybelles, ripe in December,

and sugary pears dropping soon.
Choose a tawny port, a snowman-
patterned mask, and a Beaver Moon
to make her laugh, all chased by too
      many texts and not enough calls.
      Mail her pitiless articles

on the risks of getting together.
Put money down for blustery
weather. At last try to buy her
a bird. She says no more orders,
      no more sly schemes to deliver
      pretty tunes that might outlive her.

---

at least through memory's witchery. Certainties go to ground. Once

Mother Tree

Brown-barked, lichened and peeling, *Acer rubrum*
probes with its taproot toward old clay pipes.

It remembers a century back when this house
was new, its pine stairs fragrant with distress.
A human mother used to lug laundry past
the window. Influenza swept her heart bare.

Once there were three big maples reaching
out underground, sending each other sugar,
shouting chemical warnings when hungry deer
stole up or caterpillars gnawed. One
went hollow and surgeons came with their hooked belts.
A second split in straight-line winds and smashed
the porch. This is the last, and ailing. Trash branches
snag among its living limbs. The great
gray trunk angles away. A tea-hued nest
is stranded in the lace woodpeckers made.

When my mother turned eighty and the whole family
gathered, February 2020,
I guessed what we risked to join at those long tables.
Not how the year would stretch and decay.

I want more seasons of bud, flower, samara,
but my mother is too sad to answer calls.
I research constricted visiting hours,
pack a bag halfway and leave it open.

Freud found a fairy ring. Deleuze & Guattari digress on it[13]—how

Prescriptions

To forget how a body becomes a church, doors
splintered and gasping, call on a daughter
to trickle lorazepam and morphine under the apse
of your blistered tongue. Ask this with stained-
glass hands that flicker along the bedsheet.

To leave the service, wait for the moment
your children shut their eyes and lose
themselves in music. Maybe it's your wedding. No,
you eloped with a close-mouthed man. He's gone now.
Sneak out the back, forgetting your coat.

There was a time you sat in a garden alone.
Return there. Resist mothering for a while or forever.
Sit on the grass as if it's easy to rise when you want.
The tender blades love you. A remedy
of peonies feels your shine and gives it back.

---

the doctor liked to hunt for   & they like to hunt for
edible mushrooms

First in Line for Takeoff

Undertakers rang the bell at three a.m.
It groaned like a pipe organ. I wasn't
dressed for church. My sister, in a tee
and sleep shorts, admitted two black suits.
Their shiny paisley ties reminded me
I was braless under sad-colored pajamas.
The accents were serious Jersey.
When the men clasped their hands as if
in prayer, their cufflinks flashed an epiphany.
I didn't watch them carry out the body bag.

I shouldn't have told this to the sharp dresser
who cuts my hair, but he knows about grief.
As damp curls crash, he gives me the title
for this poem. *I couldn't write it,* he says,
but that's what it feels like: parents fly off,
you're next. Jesus Christ, I say,
and he says, *What, did I offend you,*
and I say *No, poetry should*
make you swear. No one's grimmer inside
than me. My bully of a heart wears cheap
scuffed pumps and cusses like a mobster.

I rattled leftover opiates into a Ziploc
for my brother-in-law, the state trooper,
to spirit away. Everyone was a mess.

I'd ordered my mother a warm nightgown,
white with turquoise windowpanes,
when she owned only two and I ran
her washer daily to keep them clean.

---

the doctor. *But it is not the mushroom that is of interest to us,* they write,

She stepped out of her body too soon
for me, too late to skirt the agony, and what
does that say about what I'll spend for love?
The hospice nurse who certified her death
scissored off my mother's shirt
and changed her into the windowpanes
for one last trip. We thought that
was the decent thing. I padded
with shirt-scraps into the kitchen
and placed them next to the garbage bin.
I didn't want to look theatrical but
it was dark so I picked them up again
and inhaled her scent one last time.

You wonder what the undertakers
were thinking, the stylist says.

No one can guess what's in anyone's pockets.

Now that her ride has roared off
and I glimpse a gray hem of runway,
a vision comes of suitcases stowed in a cargo hold.
Alone in the row, I slide my mind into airplane mode.

---

so much as the underlying mycelium.
       This mycelium is, mycologically speaking,

The Facilities

· In the afterlife it's hard to find
      a toilet. We wander
through sun-drunk mazy
      hedges, happening on family
and friends sitting in clusters
      of generous lawn chairs,
but the nearby house, she points out,
      has too many steps
for all these old people.
      She says she prefers
the second of the flowerbeds
      where I sprinkled her ashes,
around those trillium, aren't they
      strange, in earshot of children
roaring at the zoo, but please
      stop carrying my cremains
in a tin for arthritis cream.
      For heaven's sake.
It's funny, she goes on, the pitch
      of her voice a meandering vine,
how your dreams dress me
      in what I wore to your wedding.
I worried too much about
      those arrangements. Always guessing
what other people were thinking.
      As if anything matters except
the company of birds and, close by,
      a cleanish bathroom. Hold my arm,

---

a rhizomorph—networks of associative thinking. Also

that's right. When you wear
      my earrings and they chime,
that's me, looking for a place to go.

Writing a paper as a rhizome entails reaching the point, not where

The Trial

Justice requires moss growing over the lip
of the witness box. It's not like you can stop

thinking about your mother: less the drowsy
afternoon at Jones Beach when she whispered
through a cloud of coconut scent, *You didn't know
I was pregnant?* than the overcast morning
you saw there wouldn't be another summer,
no mother smiling with her eyes closed,
head fringed like a dandelion clock.

A poem is a desk propping a gavel-handed I
with the right to judge the old woman
whose silence once cut worse than words,
who stood by and watched him hurt you,
whose best blazer drowns her now.

It's as if a sheen of salt lasted longer
than the heat of anybody's skin.
Sand freckles the page.

Forgive yourself, people say, as if brains
are courtrooms packed with men in wigs
and jurors trying to look reliable.
I got distracted by trivia. I failed
to tend her as well as she deserved.

---

one no longer says I, but
where it is no longer [hyphae are always getting longer]
                                        of any importance

Some kind soul has cracked a high window.

Remember when, loose-limbed and gritty,
you lugged wet towels back to the parking lot
and a crow swooped to steal a lock of her hair?
Your mother yelled and laughed and you
yelled and laughed and were amazed
at the fibers entangling everyone,
how a flash of wing stole something
you would have kept back, forgivably.

---

whether one says I. Language
        reticulates. Verse are folds.

Aromatic

Everyone inherits
something. A recipe,
a ring, a sureness
of being good enough,
a rhizome of feeling.

My mother and her mother
grew among paving bricks
in tenements. Their fathers
mean as dirt, like mine.

Mint survives almost anything.
My grandmother made sauce:
fistfuls loosely chopped, vinegar,
sugar, one gritty pinch of salt.

They called me the messy
one, sullen, picker of fights.
But green rootstalks sleep
in my mouth, snarled, thinking.

Two generations and even the memory
of anybody's hands is gone.
Still mint breeds untended
and blooms in spikes.
In spring, it tastes like
returning to life. In summer,
the scent bestows ease.

I are you are one be gods. Interests rhyme. Mycelium gives.
Mycelium takes. Like an essayist

Minus Time

Snow puts hush on show, possum-claw
prints in a lavender yard, a no-one-going-
anywhere crust on the road. Ruminant snow,
jumbled with gravel. Misery snow of dazzling
tenacity. Snow chokes, snow's broken,
snow is unable to imagine spring, tricky
and trickling. Snow is me. Snow chance.
Snow money in my pocket never meant
to be spent. Snow body knows the trouble
I've seen. Gung-snow in slushy treads,
freezing and creaking. Yet the streets tear up.
Gutters jingle. Despite the snow-down, winter passes—

---

mycelium breaks mess
down to sense. This is the magic I've got. Connecting through my feet

Carpenter Ant with Zombie Fungus

Some days the soil spits up toys
and teeth of broken glass.
Clay-scent and green insinuation.
Beneath, within, hyphae fizz
with information: phosphorus
for the river birch answered
by food converted from light.
Maybe what seemed haunted
is involuted. Here in the little
yard where I did not mean
to confine my life, quietness
gives acoustic space not just
to leashed dogs speaking their hearts,
not just to wrens and the outraged
catbird with her score of scolding
tones, but to a rumble I can almost
feel and chemical signals I may
respond to before I mean to,
the way a word of wonder leaps
from my tongue without leave.
Mycorrhizal conversations.
Brightly intimate seams spiking
through me the way a fungal
fruiting body erupts from an ant's
head. Mycelium knows some things
about what the dogwood strain for,
undercover, and what I dream,

I thought to a planet   but maybe the voice murmuring back

                  as organism—

world I can't call mine branching
and blooming in the sense of choosing
among histories and futures always
present, all at once, commensally.

---

was always legion—endlessly forking masses of wanting & that's why

Cloud Petition

Here is a script for a ceremony
to conduct because you do not
believe. Lay out words: gilt,
soiled, confusion, ragged. Lift
them with fog hands and sing.
People could be listening.
It's possible. Incense may smoke
and scratch your throat
but its mist does not object
to your tiredness and doubt.
So say amen. Say shantih
or whatever syllables feel good.
No matter how they taste,
their incredible testaments will
condense to rain in your mouth.

---

sentences erupt from rot & deliquesce back into it. [don't know what I'm saying

Divination

by fig leaves, by sneezes, by clouds,
    by blemishes, by wheel ruts, by fractal,
        by seeds in bird excrement, by old shoes,
by navels, by the howling of dogs, by eggs,
    by teeth, by mushrooms, by smoke, by dreams.
        Ask for understanding; you shall
not receive. Rumpology, sikidy,
    sortilege, floriography, shufflemancy, and
        for rhapsodomancy you toss a die
onto a poem. It lands on a sideways reply,
    the only kind gods ever give, but you can live by it
        if you dare to steer by a nowhere map,
by pleasure, by persimmon, by ear.

---

but will try to say it better] My mother remembered being reincarnated.

In the Belly

As a woman carries an insect, unconscious
of the sign it shapes with diplomatic footfalls
across her skin, she carries me. As a lake
lifts the sky's image, all burnished admiration, or
proffers a crushed cup, a leaf, a rainbow slick
of grease. As your network of neurochemicals
and electricity carries, through flicker but indelibly,
flame of the first death to teach you anyone
can be lost. A charred mark. Ring stain.
She carries me like a tired parent carries
a limply sleeping child, like an embossed page
carries a warning, like a gutter carries a bird's nest.
She carries everyone germinant, everyone needling
like sleet and wind, everyone starving or afraid.
Stop for a moment and feel for it as a tongue
seeks a jagged tooth, the pressure of her carrying,
and give her permission through your muscles.
Her holy day means lambing, beds of rushes,
means no more lone shouldering of a long hard year.

She also said
      when you're dead, you're dead—please scatter my ashes in a garden.

Leonids

They look like freckles on a person
with a lot of freckles, I said, and he laughed

and said, *I knew there was a reason*
I married you. The best time for viewing,

I'd read, was after midnight, so we
set out for the hill by the elementary school

at nine p.m., which is practically midnight,
and argued about where to lay the blanket,

a black one streaked with pale cat hairs.
We were getting older. We had settled

for love over could-have-beens, casting
off aspirations that would

have riven us. Meanwhile
my fingers went numb in their gloves.

The Norwegians, I told him, *say there's no*
bad weather, just bad clothes, but

my base layer is stuck in the mail.
Satellites tricked us. Stars did their thing.

[wrested & resting] Part of things. I miss her so much. I'm lonely in loss,

What's with the twinkling anyway,
he asked, and I promised to look it up.

We never saw a meteor. Instead
I began sliding downslope, my glossy

jacket launched by the slippery blanket
and me hooking an arm around his neck

then rotating sideways like the dial
on a clock, unable to unburn, I was a

meteor, icy fragment losing myself
in a view that never stops

                    & no one's gone, just enjambed
but no one's alone

Vitamin Shine

Dutchman's breeches suspect it as they air
in April sun. Virginia bluebells mull it over
as they quit the soil's closet, as I should do,

one of these lengthening days. My photoreceptors
hope for it, converting light into electrochemical
petals fluttering into my thalamus, touching

secret currents. Shimmer on water is
ovation, restoration, relation. If I dose
myself with what it knows, I can glitter, too.

& the next page illegible. For now—alternative to festering rage—

The Red Door

What trouble scratches at the red door?
Release it, not knowing. So your people
left you alone in the wood: let go.

Let go of trouble or people? No one knows.
Let not knowing go. Unclasp your words
and let them float. While exiting your body,

they may tear another hole. Don't mourn it.
Wounds open then close at an hour you don't
control. As hurt swung wide, let it heal over.

Don't adore the scar, rose token of home.
Burn the kindling you've been carrying.
Molecules of smoke shiver and let go.

---

let's concoct libations of some yeast-fermented drink for a famished
                                                    gossipy
                                                        self-obsessed

Tone Problem

Low-down ground by the stream acts joyful.
Bluebells, trillium? Get out of town with your frilled
carillon. Pink Moon, Grass Moon, Egg Moon,
there's no call to fling brilliance in this
of all springs. I can't even with such beauty.
Can't explain to the ardent lilac.
No words for love-crazed blue jays,
for the cat slinking through lemon-balm.
Calm down, iridescent mist swept
along by always-rising winds. The nerve.
The outrageous auxiliary verb: may be.

---

filthy old-growth poetry that even if it doesn't shatter its mud ceiling

Message from the Next Life
for Beth

I'm calling you from the opposite pier of the blood-bridge
which in steel-girdered insomnia I shortened to bludge
although now the moody river whispers maybe broodge.
Hot flash, misindirection, fleshiness, rust.

Apologies for making it look bad. The view doesn't suck
although it's complicated, all cat's-cradle cables blocking
what I remember as meadow, a ruckus of mockingbirds,
green creepers, meteors. Well, you know the place. After

crossing I kept dreaming of the third baby I never bore.
They talk to me in brain-beams. They and I want to conjure
an envelope of love for you to carry over the swaying deck,
sweck, derve, I can't stop recombinating so fuck

it: we'll put our backs into budging your luck. Let fate rhyme
a smidge of wish into a sleepless package delivered just in time.

---

remains willing to mulch more poems—each not-one a thallus

Return Path

The only way to pray is through my feet,
earthward, jolted in return by the fizz
of a spiking current. I never thought a circuit

would loop through me, believed I was separate,
alone, done with gods, but here it is:
I've found a way to pray. Through my feet,

I reach down. There's something animate,
mycelial, that touches me back. It's a species
of love, a thinking-spike, a zinging circuit

of energy and dirt, blood and spirit—
plutonic conversation, mostly wordless.
The way I've found to pray is through my feet,

sole bared to wooden boards, or rug, or slate,
or buggy grass, just as you want to press
skin to a beloved's, sparking a current, a circuit.

Not that earth loves me, exactly. Matter's what
matters. She wants me to return the mess
of my only body, pray from head through feet
as I sink, unthinking ash, into love's circuit.

---

of love's great hot underpoem—a spectacular tentacular brain

raising us &
　　　　scheming to dissolve us into the mycoverse

1 Ari Jumpponen qtd. in Andrea Watts, "The Recovery of Soil Fungi Following a Fire."

2 Merlin Sheldrake, *Entangled Life: How Fungi Make Our Worlds, Change Our Minds & Shape Our Futures.*

3 Ibid.

4 Anna Loewenhaupt Tsing, *The Mushroom at the End of the World: On the Possibility of Life in Capitalist Ruins.*

5 Alexander B. Belser et al., "Patient Experiences of Psilocybin-Assisted Psychotherapy."

6 Tsing, *The Mushroom at the End of the World.*

7 Eben Bayer, "The Mycelium Revolution Is Upon Us."

8 Qtd. in Louie Schwartzberg, *Fantastic Fungi.*

9 David Griffiths, "Queer Theory for Lichens."

10 Robert Macfarlane, *Underland.*

11 Qtd. in Schwartzberg, *Fantastic Fungi.*

12 Robin Wall Kimmerer, *Braiding Sweetgrass.*

13 Deleuze and Guattari, "Rhizome, Revisited: An Interpretive Walk Through *The Interpretation of Dreams.*"

ACKNOWLEDGMENTS

Warm thanks to the editors and publishers of the following journals, in which versions of these poems appear. I'm grateful for their generosity, care, and literary advocacy.

32 Poems: "Deferred"
About Place: "We Could Be"
Arkansas International: "For Metamorphosis, with Bibliomancy"
ASP Review: "Rhapsodomancy," "Smart"
Beloit Poetry Journal: "Minus Time"
Birmingham Poetry Review: "In the Belly"
Cimarron Review: "Counterphobic"
Couplet: "An Underworld," "Map Projections"
Diode: "Flammable Almanac," "Giant Tube Worm"
Ecotone: "Unsonnet," "Doubled, Briefly"
Gettysburg Review: "Sex Talk"
Guernica: "Extended Release"
Hood of Bone: "The Facilities" and "Mother Tree"
House Mountain Review: "For Evaporation of Hope, With
    Bibliomancy"
Interim: "Memorandum of Understanding"
Kenyon Review Online: "Oxidation Story"
Kestrel: "Divination," "It Is Advantageous"
Literary Matters: "Gran Torino Gigan," "Submicroscopic"
Massachusetts Review: "Message from the Next Life"

Michigan Quarterly Review: "Venus / Dodo," "Self-Portrait / Golden Shovel"

National Poetry Review: "You Know Where the Smithy Stood by the Clinkers"

Nelle: "The Red Door," "Early Cretaceous Walks Up to the Bar"

North American Review: "Particle-Wave Spell"

Notre Dame Review: "Dark Energy," "Carpenter Ant with Zombie Fungus"

One: "Convertible Moon"

Pleiades: "Peri-Aubade"

Poetry: "Prescriptions"

Smartish Pace: "In Weird Waters Now"

storySouth: "The Underside of Everything You've Loved"

SWWIM Miami: "Garden State"

Terrain: "Forecasts Can Be Invocations," "Harrowing"

Thrush: "Tone Problem"

Western Humanities Review: "Rusty Song"

Yemassee Journal: "Cloud Petition"

"Sex Talk" was featured on *Poetry Daily;* "Unsonnet" and "Deferred" appeared on *Verse Daily.* "Unsonnet" received the 2021 Bradford-Niederman Broadside Award from *Ecotone* at the University of North Carolina -Wilmington. "Return Path" also appears in the anthologies *Love Affairs at the Villa Nelle,* edited by Marilyn L. Taylor and James P. Roberts, and *Dear Human at the Edge of Time,* edited by Aileen Cassinetto, Jeremy Hoffman, and Luisa A. Igloria.

A Katharine Bakeless Nason Fellowship to the Bread Loaf Environmental Writers Workshop and a Tennessee Williams Scholarship to the Sewanee Writers Conference introduced me to wonderful people who challenged me to make these poems better. The Lenfest Endowment at W&L provided summer support.

No one writes—or publishes—alone. Several relationships haunt this book, as do the words of authors I've never met. Most of my conscious literary debts are made plain in the poems themselves, but my golden shovel source is a line from "Gay Chaps at the Bar" by Gwendolyn Brooks, and the title of "The Underside of Everything You've Loved" comes from Adrienne Rich's "Twenty-One Love Poems." The "Bibliomancy" series follows a prompt given to my class by Oliver de la Paz. The gigan is a poetic form invented by Ruth Ellen Kocher; the LaCharta was created by Laura Lamarca. Much of what I've learned about the role of enslaved labor in W&L's history I owe to Donald Gaylord, including the line "you know where the smithy stood by the clinkers," but any factual errors are mine. The "earring chandeliers" in "Memorandum of Understanding" were a gift from Hyejung Kook.

Thanks to my living mycelial network of poetic nourishment, including Ned Balbo, Jan Beatty, Cynthia Hogue, Anna Maria Hong, Luisa A. Igloria, Sally Rosen Kindred, Janet McAdams, Jane Satterfield, Elizabeth Savage, Asali Solomon, Beth Staples, Laura-Gray Street, and many others. Anna Lena Phillips Bell, Jeannine Hall Gailey, and Chris Gavaler helped enormously as I framed and reframed what became this book. I am so grateful to have a sister to root for and to feel her root for me: thank you, Claire Wheeler Kerr. Homage to the psychotropic poet Diane Seuss—I'm thrilled that she chose *Mycocosmic* as a Dorset Prize runner-up—and to Eduardo C. Corral, Denise Duhamel, and Erika Meitner for their brilliant poetry and kind endorsements. Finally, I'm very grateful to everyone at Tupelo Press who helped this mycelium fruit, especially Kristina Marie Darling, Jeffrey Levine, and David Rossitter.